ROSE in the M

Canterbury Cathedral in Story

Gloria Jarvis Smith

ISBN 978-1-899177-17-2
Copyright Gloria Jarvis Smith 2007

Published by Oyster Press, Whitstable

GLORIA JARVIS SMITH –
A Lady of many talents

By Margaret Crosland

Gloria Jarvis Smith is writing a family history which may provide the answer to an intriguing question. Just how large a part is played by heredity in the creation of a person who is not only a gifted artist, but also a poet, playwright, author and journalist? Gloria's maternal forebears were Italian. Her grandfather came from Emilia – a craftsman who worked with the great Malatesta upon the mosaics in Westminster Cathedral. Her English father was a well-known graphics artist and illustrator. Spurred on by his example Gloria trained at St Martin's School of Art in London and later at the University of Florence. She graduated with honours and later became a lecturer on historic costume and an instructor in costume drawing at the Polytechnic in Regent Street.

As a teenager she had also enjoyed writing, but it was when she married and moved to Brussels with her husband that the editor of the Brussels Times asked her for some pieces with a British flavour.

A successful painter by that time she had already won the Medaille d'Argent in Paris and the Italian Medaille d'Or. Much of her work was in permanent collections in Belgium in oils, water-colour, pastel, ink and gouache. Her portrait of Princess Paola of Liège had captured all the sweetness of her young subject, and a painting of Margaret Thatcher was said to be a favourite with that lady's husband.

Even so, the opportunity to work in another creative field was too good to miss. Gloria began to write short pieces for the Brussels Times and The Beacon (British Community News). She started with art and theatre reviews and reports on events of Belgo-British interest. Markets in Brussels and Walks in Brussels followed and tongue-in-cheek, A Look at Local Loos.

This was a surprising choice of subject for the resident painter at 'Old England' – a department store as exclusive as Fortnum and Mason, and an artist whose painting of a Frost Fair on the Thames had been exhibited at the Royal Academy and now hung beside a Rubens in the proud owner's private collection, but Gloria is a surprising person.

Quiet-voiced and modest she has a wicked sense of humour, sharp powers of observation, and a sparkling wit reserved for the most part for the enjoyment of her closest friends.

Encouraged by the success of her early writing she went on to produce short stories which were broadcast on BBC Radio 4 and the World Service. Her work also appeared in the annual exhibitions of manuscripts of l'Association Royal des Ecrivains Wallons. She then became a member of the Union Mondiale de la Presse Feminine.

On her return to England, Gloria settled in Canterbury. She was still painting, but a change of eyesight in middle age caused difficulties. She turned more and more to writing.

In 1990 she joined the SWWJ. Then she became Chairman of Canterbury Writers' Group, taking part in their annual performances of original poetry and prose at the Canterbury Festival. One of her poems, Rose in the Martydom appeared in a Tributes in Verse anthology published in Poetry Now. For four years in succession her work was read at the London Drama Festival held at the Goodrich Theatre in Putney.

Gloria's interest in history has never flagged and a project dear to her heart is to act as guide at Canterbury Cathedral, where she makes full use of her fluent French and Italian when showing groups of foreign tourists round the historic site.

The BBC has accepted one of her plays for radio, but at present the family history is her major concern. In years to come this carefully researched work may prove invaluable to social historians. It traces the life of a family of English yeomen back to mediaeval times on her father's side. The exotic flavour of Italian blood adds mystery to the story.

Many of us would like to trace our ancestry, yet few of us have the patience to search through ancient documents, picking up snippets of information from wills and parish registers. Gloria has done so, and the book, when finished, should provide a fascinating insight into the making of a writer.

*From "The Woman Writer" -
journal of The Society of Women Writers and Journalists*

Acknowledgements

My heartfelt appreciation embraces the great priors and primates, masons and engineers whose vision is responsible for the beauty and grandeur of this marvellous cathedral.

I am particularly grateful to Mrs Angela Prior, the Events Co-ordinator at the cathedral, for making it possible to reproduce many of the images in the text, and for kindly permitting other photographs to be taken by Anne Jarvis courtesy of the Dean and Chapter..

I wish to thank Angela Rose for typing up the first draft of my manuscript on computer.

Appreciation to my cousin, Anne Jarvis, for reading the manuscript and offering useful suggestions. She has my extended gratitude for undertaking the extra photography, courtesy of the Dean and Chapter.

Thanks go to the Canterbury Archaeological Trust for allowing me to reproduce some of their excellent postcards, and to Rutland County Council for the photo of Oakham Great Hall.

Most of the black and white drawings have as source The Brtitish Library.

I am grateful to The Society of Women Writers and Journalists for allowing me to reproduce from The Woman Journalist Margaret Crosland's profile of me, with special thanks to her.

Finally, I would like to express my appreciation of the many visiting groups, both French and Italian speaking, whose enthusiasm has been a source of inspiration over the years.

Contents

Introduction

"Bienvenu à la Cathédrale de Cantorbéri!"
"Benvenuti alla Chiesa di Cristo!"

Thus I would greet countless French and Italian groups over the years.
There is no better way of retaining fluency in a language. Only very
seldom was I allowed the luxury of giving a tour in my native tongue. It
was French in the morning and Italian in the afternoon – or vice versa.
No wonder I became proficient, not only in speaking, but also in facing
the challenge of trying to interpret the magnificent chiaroscuro of the
building and its history. Attempting to capture the imagination of my
listeners kept the adrenaline going. This book enables me to relive those
moments of pleasure over fifteen years or so in a series of vignettes that
I hope will convey a little of the cathedral's persona, and the
extraordinary drama that I tried to instil into those audiences, their eager
upturned faces lit by shafts of sunshine, or bathed in the sombre shades
of many a fading winter afternoon.

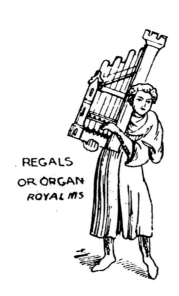

REGALS
OR ORGAN
ROYAL MS

Rose in the Martyrdom (recalled)

Photo by Anne Jarvis, courtesy of the Dean and Chapter

Canterbury Cathedral: the South Entrance; Bell Harry Tower centrally placed further east.

Photo by Anne Jarvis, courtesy of the Dean and Chapter

Well Met by Sunlight, Proud Caen Stone

"How long did the cathedral take to build?" was the question often asked by one of the knot of strangers just introduced into the Precincts and eagerly crowding round me.

"A cathedral grows over the centuries," was my reply, "as more living space is needed for the working life of the monastic community. Take Christ Church, the cathedral here, for instance – Lanfranc, William the Conqueror's first Norman archbishop, built the original Nave with the choir squeezed into its east end. But as the number of Benedictine monks increased so the next Norman archbishop, Anselm, added a choir to contain them – a choir distinct in itself beyond the Nave, with underneath, perforce, a crypt. A tiny chapel acted as a tailpiece, which in the 12th century was transformed into a second crypt, called the Eastern Crypt, larger and presenting a more worthy space to shelter Thomas Becket's shrine."

Pointing to the magnificent edifice across the way, I would illustrate my point: "Let your eye travel right along to the eastern end of the cathedral – and see how the early medieval architecture reflects that of Normandy – source of those round arches, typical of the Romanesque style.

"Whereas, coming back to the Nave opposite us, just over there – now that is more recent, having replaced its sturdy Norman original with this late 14th - early 15th century style called Perpendicular. Note that the round Norman arches had long given way to the pointed shape that the 18th century later dubbed gothic. Buttresses flying out from the wall strengthen it, allowing for more windows to let in a greater degree of light."

Time to leave the south façade with, as is so often the case in the summer months, its mellowed limestone from Caen in Normandy dazzling in the sunshine. (The medieval builders preferred to import the stone by sea thus avoiding transporting native stone only to suffer the terrible state of the English roads at the time. Caen stone was shipped to Canterbury's port of Fordwich, and finally transported the rest of the short distance by road.)

"Bell Harry Tower rising from the centre of the cathedral is 15th century, replacing the Angel Steeple of the Middle Ages, and one of the last features to be built.

"So you can see how not only a cathedral - but even a church in a minor way - will increase in size over the years, to enhance its importance and efficiency. And always remember that those builders constructed religious houses to the glory of God."

A reconstruction of the Early Norman Cathedral with a contemporary drawing of Archbishop Lanfranc

Courtesy of the Canterbury Archaeological Trust

The south face of Canterbury Cathedral, showing its flying buttresses and the immense south west window.

Photo by Anne Jarvis, courtesy of the Dean and Chapter

I GOTHIC CONSTRUCTION

TIMBER TRUSS

INFILLING

DIAGONAL RIB

TRANSVERSE RIB

BOSS

PINNACLE

FLYING BUTTRESS

CLERESTORY

BUTTRESS

TRIFORIUM

PARAPET

RIB OF DIAGONAL VAULT

NAVE ARCADE

AISLE

Ecclesiastical Architecture. The Early English buildings express freedom from the massive architectural characteristic of the Normans. This was achieved chiefly by concentrating the weight of the roof and vaulting on the butresses rather than on the walls, thus allowing larger windows and pillars with slender shafts

Source, the British Library

Onset in the Cloister

Keen for the tour proper to proceed without the extraneous noises that sometimes permeate the Nave when repair work is going on in the interior of the cathedral, I used to find it less distracting to begin in the Great Cloister round on the north side.

Skirting the cathedral, a brief stop at the west door allowed me to point out the dramatic moment on the day of a new enthronement when the lone figure of the archbishop finds the door closed against him. A knock with his crosier suffices for the door to swing open to a sense of welcome from the mass of dignitaries within. This custom is all part of the traditional procedure mapped out for the occasion.

"Whenever the archbishop is in residence," I would point out, waving towards his palace in the background, "his standard is raised. But most of the time he resides in London, at Lambeth Palace. In the capital, the centre of business, he can more easily attend to ecclesiastical matters of a more secular nature."

On into the Great Cloister. "Che bello!" How often have I heard the gasp from my Italian visitors as they caught their first glimpse of the quadrangle of dazzling ogee arches enclosing the greensward. And beyond, just appearing, rises the Romanesque pile that houses the Crypt and eastern end of the cathedral. This is a good spot to point out the diversity of period styles to architecture buffs.

It was also the moment to give a brief history: how the city grew under the Romans into a miniature Rome (with an enormous amphitheatre), and became an important stop for visiting dignitaries from the coastal ports on their way to London; how it fell into decay in the Saxon period; and how Augustine came with his forty monks on a Christian mission sent by Pope Gregory the Great in 597.

8. MURDER OF BECKET

Thomas Becket, 1118-70. As Chancellor (1152-62), he ably assisted the financial and judicial reforms of Henry II. As primate, (1162-70), his opposition to the King's religious policy led to his rejection of the Constitutions of Clarendon, his exile in France, 1164-70, and his murder in Canterbury Cathedral, 1170.

Source, the British Library

My Italian groups would lap up any references to their countrymen – such as two of the cathedral's greatest popes: Lanfranco and Anselmo. Both had been abbots of Bec in Normandy, and Lanfranc had been appointed Archbishop of Canterbury by William the Conqueror; and then his successor, William Rufus, persuaded Anselmo to follow suit.

Italians, too, can look up and see on the vault of the Cloister, among the heraldic arms, the shield of Pope John Paul II to commemorate his historic visit in 1982. To confer on him even more honour it was placed next to the shield of the martyr St Thomas Becket (with the 4 choughs). They take their place among the tapestry of arms of 15th century royalty and dignitaries wealthy enough to have donated money to the rebuilding of Cloister and Nave, which bears witness on the vault to their altruism, thus ensuring that their fame goes down to posterity. In progressing towards the Martyrdom by skirting the stone benches along the north wall of the Nave, one of those little human touches presents itself from the past.

Carved into the horizontal surface of the benches are the outlines of tiny feet and scooped out hollows for balls. This is where the novice monks of earliest times played a kind of bagatelle, and these engravings are witness to their juvenilia. It prompts murmurings of "Simpatico!" or "Sympathique!" from Italians and French alike, delighted at the story.

French pilgrims are more easily catered for with so much of the cathedral's history bound up with its Norman past. One can sense an affinity with the Saxon King Ethelbert, whose wife, Berthe, was the granddaughter of Clovis, the great Frankish king. Pagan King Ethelbert allowed his French wife to practise Christianity – "an early example of women's lib.," I always say. She must have had a big influence in persuading her husband to receive Augustine's mission in 597, resulting in his eventual conversion and baptism – not to mention the founding of a monastic community – and a cathedral that became the Mother Church of the nation and eventually the Anglican Communion worldwide.

The four knights attack Becket from a twefth century MS

Monks Distributing Charity

Source, the British Library

THE TRIAL

FRITHST○○

SANCTUARY KNOCKER

THE HUE AND CRY

JUSTICE. Under both Saxons and Normans a form of Ordeal conducted under the supervision of the Church was a common mode of trial. A criminal in danger from mob violence might obtain sanctuary, or the protection of the Church, until he could be given a legal trial.

Source, the British Library

In 1998 the installation of new central heating in the Nave brought to light the foundations of that earlier Saxon cathedral. Much to the joy of the authorities, the archaeologists have revealed that Christianity has been practised on this site for fourteen hundred years.

The door of the Martyrdom rises up at the end of the Cloister walk. On the steps leading to it King Edward I married his queen, Margaret. In fact, history buffs tread this cathedral in the footsteps of many a renowned figure from the past – not least that of Archbishop Thomas Becket who, in 1170, was hustled by his monks along the Cloister to evade the pursuing knights bent on his arrest. The north transept, now known as the Martyrdom, marks the sacred place where Thomas was murdered on 29th December 1170.

The rise of a son of a merchant family in Cheapside to become chancellor, Archbishop of Canterbury, martyr and saint was remarkable indeed.

Attracted by his personality and good looks, Henry II befriended and raised him from humble origins to the heights – in the delusion that he could bend him to his will, especially in the matter of religious policy, such as the trial of criminous clerks. This was the great bone of contention between them: at that time clerics arrested for some misdemeanour were tried in the ecclesiastical courts (considered by Henry to be too lenient); he wanted them tried under secular law. Thomas refused. This was clause 3 of the Constitutions of Clarendon, an attempt by the king to revive the ancient laws and customs of the realm instigated by William I, a century before.

Becket, assailed by hostility from king, barons and churchmen alike was forced to flee into exile in France where he remained for six years with the benediction of the French king, Louis VII. Making peace with Henry, eventually, brought about the return to Canterbury of the man whose martyrdom attracted thousands of pilgrims from all over the world until the Reformation when Henry VIII decreed that the worship

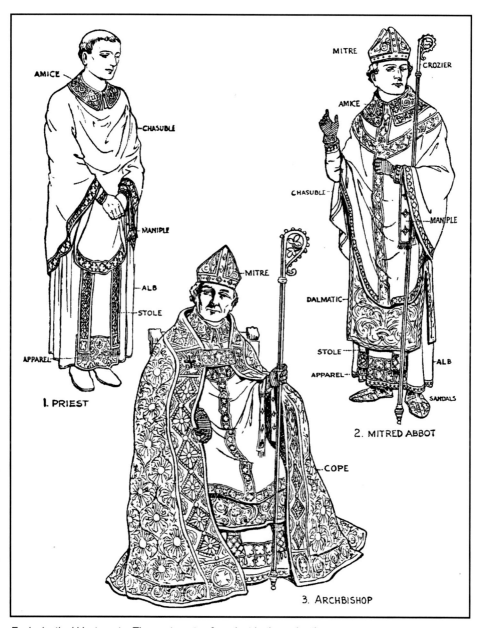

AMICE

CHASUBLE

MANIPLE

ALB

STOLE

APPAREL

I. PRIEST

MITRE

CROZIER

AMICE

CHASUBLE

MANIPLE

DALMATIC

STOLE

APPAREL

ALB

SANDALS

2. MITRED ABBOT

MITRE

COPE

3. ARCHBISHOP

*Ecclesiastical Vestments. The vestments of a priest in the order they were put on were the **Amice**, **Alb**, **Maniple**, **Stole**, and **Chasuble**. The Alb was worn by all Church officials, that of the priest being distinguished by Apparels, i.e. six pieces of emroidered linen attached to it.*

Source, the British Library

of saints was henceforth taboo. But before 1540 the pilgrimage to Canterbury vied with those of Jerusalem and Santiago di Compostela.

While in exile, Becket learned that the Archbishop of York had usurped his function by crowning Henry's son king. Henry II resided by preference in France, so he had his young heir, Prince Henry, crowned in order to act as deputy monarch in his absence. By ancient custom, the coronation and anointing of the kings of England was reserved for the Archbishop of Canterbury. With Thomas out of the land, Roger, Archbishop of York, had ousted this prerogative and by crowning the young king in Westminster Abbey had thereby flouted Becket's authority.

In his desire to punish his enemies, Thomas, on his return from exile, appealed to the pope. Papal letters of censure pronounced suspension on York and excommunication on other prelates implicated in the coronation.

When it reached the king's ears his anger knew no bounds. It was said that he had even attacked his mattress and chewed it, fulminating: "Are you all cowards to allow this man I raised from nothing to kick his heels in my face?"

At which, four knights, in order to ingratiate themselves with the king, plotted to journey to Canterbury and get Becket dead or alive.

On Christmas Day the archbishop had preached from the pulpit in what was then the great Norman Nave of the Romanesque cathedral thronged with the citizens of Canterbury – a sermon of good will to all men. Then he voiced the premonition that had begun to haunt him – of his imminent death. It made him weep, which in turn set off a paroxysm of sobbing throughout the congregation. They moaned: "Father, we shall be bereft without you!"

On the 29th December, the four knights, William de Tracy, Reginald Fitzurse, Hugh de Morville and Richard le Bret, confronted the archbishop in his palace. They had arrest in mind – with murder as a last resort.

Thomas Becket based on descriptions of the time

Seal of Becket

Source, the British Library

A violent argument ensued. Ominously, they left to retrieve their armour from a mulberry tree in the garden, to return with their swords, only to find Becket and his circle of clerics gone to celebrate vespers.

The monks had managed to hustle their archbishop along the Cloister and into the north-west transept housing the Chapel of St Benedict that later became the Martyrdom. Above was the Chapel of St Blaise borne on a tribune.

The Altar of the Sword's Point in the Martyrdom

Photo Anne Jarvis by courtesy of the Dean and Chapter

Becket was mounting the flight of steps to the Choir. His order to unbolt the door so as "not to turn the house of God into a fortress" allowed the four knights to burst in below, shouting: "Where is the traitor Thomas Becket?"

"I am no traitor!" was the archbishop's proud reply, "but a priest of God!" He descended and set himself against the great Norman pillar to face his adversaries.

Graphic written accounts by some of the monks who were shocked bystanders that late winter afternoon in the Chapel of St Benedict describe the horrific event that followed – which assassin struck which blow and what words were exchanged in the fracas, full of insults and recriminations.

Most of the accounts tally save for a few minor details. Visitors are always carried away by the chilling commentary of the guide – especially the French tourists on hearing the martyr's words that invoke France's patron saint: "To God and to the blessed Virgin Mary, to the blessed Martyr St Denis of France...I commend my spirit and the cause of the Church." At which, he managed to fall with his clothing arranged gracefully round him.

The Gallic groups who have listened open-mouthed to the dramatic narrative cannot help but feel affinity with the man who, because of his parents' provenance from Rouen, was in essence French.

In fact, such is their reverence, I have seen some Catholics linger to kneel and say a prayer before the Altar of the Sword's Point, recalling the pilgrimages of the Middle Ages.

The Altar of the Sword's Point is the great feature of that sacred place. The simple altar is overhung on the wall behind by a sculpture in bronze, symbolic in concept, to represent the point of the sword which was broken off when dashed on the paving stone in the murder. The original was eventually placed on the altar, to be kissed by the pilgrims on entry, before going down to the shrine. This continued until all saints' relics were destroyed as decreed by Henry VIII at the Reformation.

Roses and Lilies

A few years after the murder, Garnier of Pont-Sainte-Maxence, poet, contemporary and biographer of Thomas Becket, wrote of his martyrdom: "Anyone who saw the blood and the brains fall and lie mingled on the stone floor might have thought of roses and lilies, for he would have seen the blood showing red among the white brains, and the brains gleaming white against the red blood."

Who can forget the wonderful floral exhibition that transformed Canterbury Cathedral in October 1997? Created by the National Association of Flower Arrangement Societies (NAFAS), and entitled "Christian Beginnings", it formed part of the Saint Augustine Celebrations. Each part of the cathedral was given a floral design individually conceived to fit the setting.

Whoever was responsible for the floral design in the Martyrdom showed utter genius: the display of red roses crimson and carmine, entwined with a spray of lilies, cascading from the Altar of the Sword's Point evoked so poignantly the words of Garnier of Pont-Sainte-Maxence.

Perhaps some of my readers will consider that I have overplayed the story of Thomas Becket when the tour is compressed into one and a half hours. But I know from experience that people want to know the "whys and wherefores" – and thus how the quarrel between Henry II and his archbishop came about. And of course it takes time. Besides, it is fascinating to ponder the change in a man hedonistic by nature, but capable of assuming great piety. Previously, as chancellor at the royal court, he had been a lover of fashion and fine food, with prowess at hunting and war, with skill at falconry, and who cut a dashing figure striding along in sumptuous clothes, a tame wolf at his heels. But he had had a complete spiritual turn around later as archbishop, in secret wearing a hair shirt and breeches (crawling with vermin) only temporarily removed for daily flagellation. It showed the ascetic he had become – and how much his physical suffering could endure.

It must be remembered that the north-west transept housing the present day Martyrdom underwent a transformation architecturally from Norman to Perpendicular when rebuilt between 1432 and 1458. This was due to the rebuilding of the Nave (begun in 1375 approximately) which was not completed for one hundred and fifty years. And so the massive Norman pillar against which Thomas had stood steadfast in the face of his assassins had to go. Reluctantly the monks agreed to the change. They little realised that within a century the reverencing of saints would be outlawed by Henry VIII and Thomas Becket considered a traitor to the throne. Yet in this modern age his sainthood prevails. Pope John Paul II prayed before the Altar of the Sword's Point alongside Archbishop Runcie in 1982. No one heard their prayers, but they were most likely for the peace of the world and for understanding between the two churches.

Canterbury at the time of St Thomas Becket::
the Cathedral Precincts and the City in the 12th Century.

Courtesy of the Canterbury Archaeological Trust

Rose in the Martyrdom

When I remember that rose winter rose
Laid on the paving stone that bears the name
Of Thomas …
I, too, can share the sentiment of joy
Borne in that goodly pilgrim's heart
Who placed it there.
In half an hour or so that rose was gone,
Swept up by some young verger, I'll be bound,
'Fraid lest a cult be set in motion as of old,
And prompt a greater flood of pilgrims to our town
To venerate the hallowed martyr, Becket.

Gloria Jarvis Smith
(From Tributes in Verse, an anthology, 1993)

Photo by Anne Jarvis courtesy of the Dean and Chapter

Photo by Anne Jarvis courtesy of the Dean and Chapter

The Legacy of Anselm and Ernulph

Then, down a flight of steps to the Western Crypt, we follow in the footsteps of the early medieval pilgrims – and, while intimating that "from now on we are in Norman country," I would point out the diaper pattern of the walls that marked our descent.

Archbishop Anselm developed the Western Crypt through his exceedingly able abbot, Ernulph, from 1098 till 1130. It emerged logically underneath Anselm's introduction of a Choir above – up till then the Choir had been accommodated as an extension beyond Lanfranc's Nave until the latter space could no longer contain the increase in numbers of the Benedictine community.

Photo by courtesy of the Dean and Chapter

Detail of the painted ceiling and eastern end of the Chapel of Our Lady Undercroft

Photo by courtesy of the Dean and Chapter

One can describe this, the largest crypt in Britain, as a church in itself, with aisles flanked by columns – and, unusually for a crypt, it is situated above basement level. The light filtering through the few windows lends a mysterious atmosphere to this holy place where quietness reigns.

The masterpieces – chef d'oeuvres to the French – are the decorated shafts and fantastic capitals of the pillars (to be discussed later during the course of this official itinerary).

So, proceeding towards the east, at the end of the processional side aisle, the recently restored north side of the Chapel of Our Lady Undercroft comes into view; it is a must for the eyes of the visitor. Perceived through Gothic screens, it beguiles many an admiring onlooker who learns that it was a gift from the Black Prince, who himself wished to be buried in this chapel, but the monks considered the Trinity Chapel as more fitting.

The blue ground of the ceiling of Our Lady Undercroft is decorated with gilded suns and stars, the latter originally covered with pieces of glass that scintillated in the candlelight (particularly intriguing for those with an imaginative disposition). These decorations, executed in the fresco technique, underwent repainting over the medieval period from the 12th to the 15th centuries.

Just behind the little chapel, and reinforcing the Eastern Crypt that we are about to come to, stand two stout Norman columns equidistant from one another at each end of the ambulatory. They were brought from Anselm's Choir after the fire in 1174, and are a reminder of how his cathedral must have looked.

The Eastern Crypt, a masterpiece of Early English architecture, scene of the first shrine with its many miracles happening around it. Note the lights of the watching chamber over the entrance, where two monks surveyed the shrine below (between two pillars of purbeck marble). An Italian priest, an amateur geologist, pointed out that "as insects would be trapped in the Purbeck marble, they would be the oldest part of the cathedral".

Photo by Anne Jarvis, courtesy of the Dean and Chapter

Early English Gothic in All its Purity

On the left hand wall of the ambulatory, round the back of the Chapel of Our Lady Undercroft, is a pictorial evocation of Becket's first shrine as it must have appeared in the small Norman chapel that predates the present Eastern Crypt - apparent through its entrance ahead. The Norman chapel was razed, but the shrine protected by a shed as the Eastern Crypt went ahead with construction. Its creator was William the Englishman, who was also the architect of the newly-designed Trinity Chapel above. Incidentally, he also completed the Choir begun by William of Sens that replaced Anselm's.

Built between 1179 and 1184, the Eastern Crypt was meant to lend a more glorious setting to Becket's shrine. For by then the pilgrimage to Canterbury had become just as significant as those to the Holy Land and San Compostella in Spain.

Photo by Anne Jarvis, courtesy of the Dean and Chapter

The picture shows the coffin encased in a stone structure with apertures at the sides in which pilgrims thrust their heads so as to be as close to the saint as possible. It was situated between pillars of Purbeck marble lining the central aisle. To step across the medieval tiles at the entrance to the Eastern Crypt suddenly brings one face to face with Early English Gothic architecture, quite unadulterated in its original purity.

The window of the Wax Chamber still looks down on the empty space where the shrine had stood, guarded by two priests at the window, as pilgrims from every part of Christendom deposited their gifts around the tomb. Many of those gifts were of inestimable value, such as Louis VII's great ruby ring, dubbed the Régale of France. It was one of the prizes filched after the Dissolution of the Monasteries by Henry VIII when twenty-six cartloads of valuables left the cathedral for the king's coffers. One of Holbein's portraits shows Henry wearing the Régale of France on his thumb. He eventually presented it to his daughter, Mary, who threaded it on a necklace, carelessly it would seem, as it was lost on a hunting expedition. My French visitors were amused to hear me say: "Somewhere under an English forest lies hidden in the undergrowth the Régale of France!" Lucky acquisition for the chance finder!

In 1174 Henry II came as penitent pilgrim to the shrine, barefoot and clothed in deep humility as a beggar. Prostrating himself before the tomb, he was to fast all night, after ordering the monks to give him countless lashes of the whip. The next day he celebrated mass, and feeling, no doubt, that the great burden of conscience had been lifted from his shoulders, he left in better mood for London. He was back in the pope's good books.

At the eastern end of the Crypt is the lower storey or undercroft of the Corona that occupies the cathedral above; this part of the Eastern Crypt houses the charming little Chapel of Jesus and Mary – so called because of its ceiling decorated with letters M (for Mary the Mother of Christ) and the crowned I (initial for the Latin J in Jesus). Thanks to the wonders of modern science these letters were temporarily removed during the 20th century for a damp proof layer to be laid before being put back. This never failed to impress my listeners, nor the fact that a visiting group with a Catholic priest is permitted to celebrate mass in the chapel, and, being in view of the beautiful 13th century window, such an event must be blessed with pictorial appeal. But then the ecumenical message is strong in the cathedral: incense is sometimes wafted along its aisles, while candles, ready for the visitors to light, convey to the foreigners a feeling of home.

On leaving the Eastern Crypt in the southern corner, a series of medieval graffiti catches the attention on either side of the exit. Etched into the walls of Caen stone, the stylised head of a stern Christ stares through the protective glass panels – as do other biblical subjects expressed in linear form. Alongside are two immense columns of Saxon origin brought from Reculver.

The ceiling of the Chapel of Jesus and Mary

Photo by courtesy of the Dean and Chapter

Romanesque wall paintings in St Gabriel's Chapel, with a pillar with Romanesque capital. The murals show scenes from the life of St John the Baptist.

Photos by Anne Jarvis, courtesy of the Dean and Chapter

The Intimacy of St Gabriel's Chapel

Through the exit into the ambulatory of the Western Crypt one finds, facing the south side of Our Lady Undercroft, the entrance to St Gabriel's Chapel. There, its unretouched Norman capitals sporting fabled beasts – and the 12th century fresco ahead – create a lovely oasis to linger in.

This fresco in the apse at the eastern end depicts the life of St John the Baptist; it is particularly prized as being one of the finest 12th century frescos in northern Europe. The primitive expressiveness lends charm. Originally the apse was blocked off to be discovered comparatively recently. The damp-free setting of the interior wall would explain the fresco's survival, for its clarity fades away as it approaches the outer wall which is more disposed to erosion by damp.

Because it was hidden away it escaped the ravages of the Reformation and the Civil War. The original motif of the monks after Becket's murder to have a bolt hole for valuables had acted as safeguard. The fresco reveals an array of colours ranging from vermilion to lapiz lazuli to malachite and gold leaf – an expensive palette indeed.

Capital at Twyford Church by one of the artisan carvers of Canterbury's Western Crypt.

Courtesy of Rutland County Council

From a capital in the Western Crypt this stern lion stares out at you.

Photo by Anne Jarvis, courtesy of the Dean and Chapter

A Menagerie of Masterpieces
to Dazzle the Eye

Back into the interior of the Western Crypt proper, one can gaze into the Chapel of Our Lady Undercroft where there are seats for quiet meditation. An altar has been there since 1130. The chapel is presided over by the statue of the Virgin, a modern replica of the 17th century Portuguese statue in ivory, which in turn had replaced the one in solid silver of the Middle Ages. The present version was sculpted by an Anglican nun inspired by the ivory statue after the theft during a service in the Nave – before strict security measures were brought in and the Crypt locked during the divine offices.

Both altar and screen date from 1370 – a gift of the Black Prince, who willed that his body should be buried before the altar. But, at his demise, the monks considered the Trinity Chapel a more splendid setting for such a heroic royal personage.

The aisles of the Western Crypt are flanked by pillars whose capitals rank as the masterpieces of the Norman carvers, who probably worked on them from around 1100 onwards. Ornamenting capital and shaft alternately, these imaginative artisans invested the in-between capitals with a menagerie of dragons, wyverns and an amphisbaena – inspired, no doubt, by the bestiary pattern books of the time; the whole gives quite a pagan flavour. But by then the clergy had the wisdom to realise that, despite the centuries since Augustine, the populace still nurtured some pagan leanings within their Christian faith, therefore it is quite natural to find Celtic and druidical symbolism in the teeming menagerie of griffons, eagles, serpents, dogs, intertwined with lush vegetation and the oak and mistletoe. The format is either carved capital or shaft – but not both. Some capitals show Celtic influence in, for example, the flowing scrolls of tongues poking out to affright the enemy, as the custom was in medieval times.

As we process along the central aisle, suddenly a magnificent stylised lion stares sternly out, recalling the symbolism of the Middle East. Trade brought into the country fabrics with fabulous designs to inspire and be copied. Who can fail to be amused by two juggler/acrobats – perceived by the carver in the streets of Canterbury, no doubt?

Considering the unsophisticated tools they had then, these carvings show the extraordinary skill of those artisans who had come over from Normandy to seek work here – and further afield in England. In fact I came across the fruits of their labour in the great hall of Oakham Castle in Rutlandshire, the carved pillars showing the same skill. The capitals in Canterbury were carved not later than 1178 – when there was no longer any work for them; funds had dried up by 1183, and as the cathedral refurbishing was completed in 1184, the craftsmen had to seek work elsewhere, such as at churches in Grantham, Lincolnshire and Twyford, Leicestershire.

Interior of the Great Hall, Oakham Castle, showing the carved capitals which are reminiscent of those in Canterbury's Western Crypt. (The blocked doorways once led to the kitchens). Courtesy of the Libraries and Museums, Rutland Counry Council

Franglais

The west end of the Western Crypt is partitioned off as the Treasury housing an exhibition of chalices and other memorabilia from the cathedral and its diocese. The western wall at the back is what remains of Lanfranc's cathedral, with rubble from the previous Saxon church incorporated in its masonry .

As one contemplates the rough hewn masonry, it is almost possible to hear the voices of the builders of 1070-77, with the strains of Anglo-Saxon and Norman mingling into a kind of "franglais" of long ago. For this part of the Crypt of Lanfranc's church extended out into the present Crypt where it is marked on the floor with a thin semi-circular line of metal to outline one of Lanfranc's apses.

Opposite the Treasury stands the pillar with unfinished capital terminating the right hand central aisle. Its incompleteness shows that the whole, both capital and shaft, were done in one piece in situ.

The north-eastern transept of the Western Crypt houses the Chapels of St Nicholas and St Mary Magdalene, with their beautiful stained glass windows. There are two tombs under slabs on the floor which arouse curiosity. One is supposedly of the cleric Edward Grim, whose arm was almost severed during his attempt to ward off the blows rained on Becket. Some believe that one of the graves could hold the bones of the martyr himself if his corpse had been whisked out of the shrine before the commissioners arrived, to be secretly buried somewhere in the cathedral. In 1956 Archdeacon Julian Bickersteth and Canon John Shirley, both colleagues on the Chapter, donated the red sanctuary lamp in the Chapel of St Mary Magdalene (red being the symbolic colour of martyrdom). Whether they had special knowledge is unknown. A coterie has since sprung up, who pray there twice a year, in the belief that it is Becket's resting place.

The transept on the south side was converted into the Black Prince's Chantry in 1363, now in use as the French Protestant Church. The French Walloon refugees were allowed to take over the Western Crypt in 1575 and their descendants have continued to worship there in the Black Prince's Chantry at 3pm every Sunday. In the old days a sermon could take up to four hours. The service is still celebrated in French.

A French tourist conjectured that the Black Prince was about six feet in height, (Trinity Chapel)

Photo by Anne Jarvis courtesy of the Dean and Chapter

On Their Knees in Wonder

Casting a final glance at the Western Crypt as it lies quietly wreathed in shadow, the groups took their leave through the exit in the south-west corner and started the climb up through to the Trinity Chapel and Corona. It is ascent all the way till arrival at the Pilgrims' Steps marks the final flight, indented by the knees of the penitents as they climbed in awe of the saint they had come to venerate.

Their goal was Becket's shrine, translated from the Western Crypt to the newly rebuilt Trinity Chapel that had been consecrated in 1220 in the presence of King Henry III and the great and the good of the Church of England and France. For had not this worthy saint by his death enriched the cathedral beyond the monastic community's wildest dreams? That is why his body had been translated to this venerable setting made beautiful in his honour.

Sometimes today's school children emulate those distant pilgrims and climb the last flight on their knees to find out just how uncomfortable it could be. If they cast their minds back to medieval times they would see a couple of monks raising the wooden cover off the shrine – to reveal it gleaming and gorgeous with gold, silver and precious stones donated by wealthy pilgrims of yesteryear in grateful anticipation of the miracle each craved. Those struggling ever upwards, at last would lift their heads to behold the spectacle, stunned at its brilliance. As the cover was lifted its attachment of little bells would tinkle away in joyous greeting.

Now only a burning candle marks the sacred spot that was the culmination of the pilgrimage. The pavement of Cosmati mosaic, gifted by Archbishop Stephen Langton, is encircled by gorgeous columns of a greenish pinkish marble from Sicily, which was sent by the contemporary pope to enhance the holy place. The Trinity was beloved by Becket – and, later, the Black Prince, too.

The Tomb of the Black Prince, with two of the Miracle Windows beyond.

Photo by Anne Jarvis courtesy of the Dean and Chapter

Close to the sacred site two royal personages are entombed. On the south side is the Black Prince, Edward Prince of Wales, about six feet in height, a Frenchman in one of my groups conjectured from his effigy. His victories always had to be glossed over in deference to French pride, I judged, perhaps unfairly.

The French were fascinated by the fact that the poem encircling the tomb is in Old French – said to be the prince's favourite verse. Norman French was still spoken in court circles till just beyond this period when English had become the norm throughout the land. The Black Prince's beloved bulldog lies at his feet, the Lion of Royalty at his head; the whole effigy is in gilded brass.

This champion of English chivalry was buried with great pomp. The enamelled shields on the sides of the tomb bear the arms of England, and his three feathers with the words "Ich Dien" (I serve) – this last having been captured on the field of battle when wrested from the King of Bohemia. Above is a canopy depicting the Holy Trinity well-loved by the prince, and overhung by copies of his Achievements – armorial bearings in recognition of military feats. The originals are protected under glass at the foot of the Pilgrims' Steps: a helm with its crest, a leopard upon cap of maintenance; the jupon or surcoat; the shield; the scabbard with buckle and part belt; the gauntlets. Only the sword is missing. The copies above the tomb are 20th century, made in the armoury of the Tower of London.

Archbishop Sudbury conducted the funeral by singing the pontifical requiem in the presence of the court and English and French bishops. A wrought iron grille was placed around the tomb; only the most important people were allowed inside.

In the north and south aisles a series of masterpieces known as the Miracle Windows look down on the Trinity Chapel. Its creators were artisans whose previous handiwork enhances the Cathedral of Sens. The miracles that happened in the Eastern Crypt come alive in the vivid stained glass, especially the singular intense blue.

Miracle Window: King Louis VII dreams of Becket's promise of a miracle to cure his son.

Photo by Anne Jarvis courtesy of the Dean and Chapter

Effigies of King Henry IV and his Queen, Joan of Navarre

Photo by courtesy of the Dean and Chapter

William the Conqueror silver penny struck by the Canterbury moneyar WINDEDI in c. 1086. Found beneath 41 St Georges Street in 1985. The mint was in the vicinity of the Mint Yard in Northgate. Courtesy of the Canterbury Archaeological Trust

I used to point out to the French the miracle associated with King Louis VII of France, who is depicted in bed (distinguishable by his crown) dreaming that Becket appears to him, promising that if he will go and do penance at his shrine, he will cure his son who lies gravely ill. Louis follows the saint's counsel and in gratitude donates the ring with the enormous ruby – the Régale of France.

The Miracle Windows on this, the north side, look down on another royal personage, King Henry IV (died 1413), uncle of the Black Prince whose son, Richard II, he deposed. His recumbent effigy alongside his wife, Joan of Navarre, lie sculptured in alabaster wearing striking crowns of oak leaves and fleur de lys. It was discovered in the 19th century that the effigy bore a close resemblance to the king, for there had been some doubt as to whether it actually was his body in the tomb. The legend persisted that when he was brought by sea from Westminster a storm had blown up and that the superstitious sailors, fearful about having a corpse aboard, might have consigned it to the waves.

But when the tomb was opened it was found that the body had been perfectly preserved in the airtight enclosure. The king's hair and beard of a "deep russet colour" gave genuine proof of his identity. It was a split second revelation, for, with exposure to air, the body fell to dust.

Close by is the figure of Nicholas Wotton, the first dean after the Reformation, kneeling over his tomb. Renaissance in character, its beautiful carving perhaps emphasising the new movement: the New Foundation of Dean and Chapter.

On the other side of the Trinity Chapel is the tomb of Archbishop Hubert Walter (died 1193) – the archbishop whose arrival when Bishop of Salisbury at the Crusades turned the army of swearing, gambling English troops into a well-behaved force. It is thought that one of the sculptured heads around the tomb might be that of Saladin, especially as there had been a certain empathy between the two men.

Tomb of Hubert Walter, reputed head of Saladin front extreme left.

Photo by Anne Jarvis, courtesy of the Dean and Chapter

Tomb of Hubert Walter. The reputed head of Saladin on extreme left.

Photo by Anne Jarvis courtesy of the Dean and Chapter

Henry IV's Chantry Chapel with the fan/vaulting, alongside his tomb

Photo by courtesy of the Dean and Chapter

The tomb is considered to be similar to the one Becket might have been buried in. A crescent of gilded wood, which was perhaps brought back from the Crusades in order to hang over St. Thomas's shrine, still remains in its original position above the site, now marked by a burning candle.

Another miracle I used to point out has a surprising medical flavour. It can be found high in the south-facing window overlooking the tomb of the Black Prince, and shows perhaps the earliest example of doctors examining urine in a phial. They are beside a sick patient who is lying, one imagines, in the cathedral Infirmary. The monk in question was evidently being cured by the miracle that he had prayed for.

On the north side of the Trinity Chapel, alongside the tomb of Henry IV and his queen, an exquisite Chantry Chapel has been built out into the Cloister, at the request of the king. It is where he wished priests to sing daily mass for his soul after his death. It is dedicated to Edward the Confessor. The roof is the earliest example of fan vaulting in the cathedral.

Miracle Window, Trinity Chapel showing earliest example of doctors examining a patient's urine in a phial.

Photo by Anne Jarvis courtesy of the Dean and Chapter

The Redemption window in the Corona

Photo by courtesy of the Dean and Chapter

Becket's Crown

Beyond the Trinity Chapel is the tail of this great cathedral – the Corona – which is also called the Chapel of the Saints and Martyrs of Our Time, some of whom have their lives and deaths commemorated in the albums on display before the entrance. Here, in the chapel, Archbishop Runcie and Pope John Paul II celebrated mass together during his famous visit in 1982. Cardinal Reginald Pole, the Catholic archbishop under Mary is buried here. The Redemption window looks down, its wonderful stained glass showing Crucifixion, Resurrection and Ascension. It is here that a piece of the crown of Becket's head hung as a relic, in a silver receptacle, before the Reformation.

On leaving the Trinity Chapel one's eye is caught by the central floor decoration showing roundels with the signs of the zodiac and months of the year, but it only feels the touch of human feet when a very significant function is taking place – such as the enthronement of an archbishop when he is crowned here in St. Augustine's Chair. Although this marble throne does not date from Augustine's time, it is about eight hundred years old and stands in splendid isolation, overlooking the High Altar in the Sanctuary below.

The perfect vantage point to view the extent of the cathedral is just behind the site of Becket's shrine. From there the ascending levels rise impressively like a crescendo – from Nave to Choir, to Sanctuary, to Trinity Chapel and culminating in Becket's pre-Reformation shrine, where a candle now burns night and day.

SHRINE OF BECKET
FROM A WINDOW IN
CANTERBURY CATHEDRAL

Source, the British Library

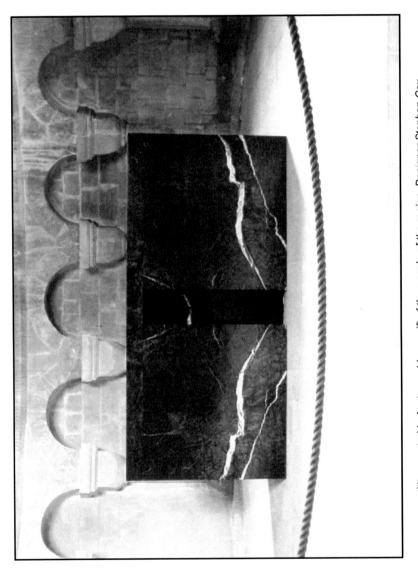

Altar created in Aosta marble - a gift of the people of the region. Designer Stephen Cox

Photo by Anne Jarvis courtesy of the Dean and Chapter

Majesty in St Anselm's Chapel

Just off the south-east aisle, at the foot of the Pilgrims' Steps, is the entrance to the chapel dedicated to St Anselm where his body is interred. One of my Italian groups was blessed with a priest who hailed from Aosta, Anselm's birthplace, and so they were keen to see the strip of marble from those parts sporting Anselm's name carved on it over his grave.

When I mentioned Anselm's reluctance to come to Canterbury, the priest was quite bemused by the fact that a man of such natural humility and gentleness had resisted the appointment for so long. But as I explained, England was a country then which Anselm, like Lanfranc before him, considered somewhat rough and unenlightened; despite the fact that he was already in a friendly relationship with the religious community of Canterbury, yet in comparison with France he felt more at home in his role of Abbot of Bec in Normandy, where he had established a seat of learning. "Will you yoke me, a weak old sheep, with that fierce young bull, the King of England?" the abbot exclaimed of William Rufus, who had inherited the Conqueror's hot temper.

Eventually, after reluctantly agreeing to be archbishop, he was enthroned at Canterbury in September 1093. Anselm met the king's aggressive approach with equal firmness of will, absenting himself on occasion from the country to travel to Rome and France, even going into exile for a time – having given offence to the king by his outspokenness. He had gone counter to the monarch's sole right of recognition of the pope asserted by the Conqueror. Anselm acknowledged Urban as pope, whereas William Rufus did not, thus putting them both in conflict with one another.

Since the visit of the priest from Aosta, Anselm's compatriot, there has been an important acquisition to the chapel: a special altar created in Aosta marble, a gift from the people of the region Autonoma Valle D'Aosta. It was consecrated at a special service on 21st April

2006 by the most Reverend and Rt. Hon. Rowan Williams, in the presence of the Bishop of Aosta, Monsignor Giuseppe Anfossi, with also present the Father Abbot and Mother Prioress of Bec – the place where the erudite Anselm had so happily officiated, the quality of his learning having drawn in scholars from all parts of the world.

Anselm's literary legacy lies in his Prayer and Meditations. His most famous work was a study of the Incarnation, while his letters bear testimony to him as a theologian and philosopher. Despite frequent absences, Anselm did not neglect his duties at Canterbury, and through successive priors Conrad and Ernulph, he ruled well. We know him from priory monk Eadmer, his disciple, whose life history of his friend reveals the man.

We have to thank Anselm for enlarging the cathedral with the addition of Romanesque Choir (predating the present one) above his fabulous Western Crypt. Sadly, he did not live to see for himself the consecration of the Choir, for he died in 1109. Romanesque, it was considered an architectural feat with eastern transepts and chapels. Eventually his body was moved from the Nave to the Chapel of St Peter and St Paul, now the Chapel of St Anselm.

Anselm would have appreciated the miniature 12th century fresco of St Paul shaking off the viper high up on the east wall of the apse. This owes its preservation to the fact that it had been hidden for centuries by an interior buttress (since replaced by an exterior one).

And of course, the Decorated window enhances this little chapel, the stained glass by Clayton and Bell, towards the end of the 19th century.

But Anselm would be impressed by the splendid altar. Designed by the sculptor, Stephen Cox, "the Altar's dark symmetric simplicity lies in stark contrast to the pale curving stone of the chapel", as so aptly explained in the text alongside. The striking black and white markings of the marble do indeed take one's breath away – testimony to the majesty of the mountainous regions of Aosta and the close links between Canterbury and the saint's roots.

The Viking raid on Canterbury in c. 1011; an imaginative reconstruction with the Anglo-Saxon Cathedral in the background (whose foundations lie under the present Christ Church).

Archbishop Alphege (later canonised) was taken by the Danes to Greenwich as hostage and beaten to death with oxbones by his drunken guards.

The Saxon Cathedral was ransacked by the Danes but rebuilt and the body of St Alphege returned to Canterbury during the reign of King Canute after 1023.

Thence the shrines of St Alphege and St Dunstan assumed great importance until demolished during the Reformation.

Courtesy of the Canterbury Archaeological Trust

The Nave stretching towards the east in the last throes of Gothic: the Perpendicular style. See how the columns soar, suggesting the medieval mind: ever reaching upwards towards heaven.

Photo by Anne Jarvis, courtesy of the Dean and Chapter

Through Choir to Fan Vaulting:
the Pièce de Résistance – the Nave

Out in the south-east transept let us not forget the Bossanyi windows named after the creator who was commissioned to do them by Dean Hewlett Johnson at the end of World War II.

Their brightness and stylisation sometimes displease being in stark contrast to the medieval concept elsewhere. But sunshine streaming through the stained glass makes the figure of Christ glow as he blesses the children of all nations, while the triumph of good over evil lights up the other window.

Crossing over the south-eastern aisle to enter the Choir, the central boss of the Paschal Lamb and Flag comes into view. It was perhaps being carved by the master mason, William of Sens, from his position on the scaffolding, where he had been superintending the great arch of the crossing. When the scaffolding collapsed he fell, suffering such severe injuries he was invalided to France – leaving the door open for William the Englishman to take over and improve on his master's vision. Easter 1180 saw the reopening of the Choir.

The beautiful carved stone screens of Gothic arches that flank the Choir to its western end were originally hung with tapestries. These were banished during the desecration by the Puritans in the 17th century and sold to Aix-en-Provence where they still take pride of place in the cathedral there.

On leaving the Choir at the western exit through the fine wrought iron gates, it was always with feeling that I would announce to my groups: "To my mind, the pièce de résistance of the cathedral is this Nave stretching before us in the last throes of Gothic, called the Perpendicular style. See how the columns soar; they suggest the medieval mind – ever reaching upwards towards heaven and yearning for God in his mercy."

First, Look up at Bell Harry

Craning our heads to take in the Bell Harry Tower centrally situated between Choir and Nave, the marvellous fan vaulting takes one's breath away. The whole conception was that of John Wastell between 1494 and 1497. He designed the tower in brick (not long come into fashion), but cased in stone to match the rest of the cathedral. The fan vaulting was a trial run for that of King's College Chapel, Cambridge. Unseen, far above the fan vaulting is a big treadmill used for hauling up the masonry during construction, and still employed today when TV equipment is required for some big event. Under Bell Harry is the Pulpitum rising in the platform space that descends in a flight of steps to the Nave.

The Pulpitum Screen, separating Choir from Nave, is distinguished by the full length sculptures of six kings. On the left hand side of the entrance to the Choir the kings Henry V, Richard II and Ethelbert; on the right hand side Edward the Confessor, Henry IV and Henry VI. The statues have been attributed to the sculptor, Massingham III, and dated between 1391 and 1411.

From the raised vantage point of the Pulpitum platform the eye takes in the Nave, one of the most recent edifices to enhance this marvellous cathedral, majestically replacing Lanfranc's, in the late 14th - early 15th centuries.

His had been based on the Church of St Etienne at Caen, with Romanesque arches gracing the aisles. Before that, the Saxon church, said to have been the largest of its kind in Europe, was dominant when Lanfranc set foot in 1067 to discover Archbishop Stigand and his monks, huddled in trepidation round the shrines of St Dunstan and St Alphege at the eastern end. The Saxon church was destroyed by fire soon after, probably by arson, and Lanfranc's began to rise as a Romanesque model in limestone (shipped from Caen). The present example of late Gothic architecture was completed in 1405, though below its paving stones are still the remains of Lanfranc's cathedral, and, below that, the Saxon church. The new vault gave the finishing touch – ribbed, with linking liernes (that is, short-ribs connecting bosses and intersections of vaulting-ribs). They give a wonderful delicate effect. The head of its great author, Henry Yveley, can be seen carved on a boss in the Cloister vault – that whole area redesigned by his pupil, Lote.

The symbolic Compass Rose on the floor of the eastern end of the Nave points to the spread of the Anglican Communion throughout the world. Standing on a plinth of marble, the beautiful Font (with its wooden cover) is decorated with apostles and the arms of Charles I. The Font has been through vicissitudes before and during the Civil War. But the broken pieces were gathered up and hidden until, at the Restoration, they were put together again.

Canterbury's West Gate, after its 1370-90 reconstruction. The pilgrims must have always trod their way from London to Becket's shrine over the self-same drawbridge.

Courtesy of the Canterbury Archaeological Trust

Adam Delves, showing an early interest in anatomy.

Photo by courtesy of the Dean and Chapter

As Adam Delves

Adam delves in the Garden of Eden is depicted in the stained glass of the west window of the Nave. Having been moved from its original position in the clerestory of the Choir, this 12th century panel takes pride of place in the Nave – for it is so highly prized as to be available for loan to exhibitions of stained glass that crop up throughout the world from time to time.

It is part of a series of portraits of Christ's ancestors: Old Testament figures such as Enoch and Methusala, once also in the clerestory of the Choir, but which now give vitality to the great window in the south-west transept.

The figure of Adam by this 12th century artisan shows an early interest in human anatomy, the naked body being exposed above the lower covering of animal skin (hooves still attached). This panel was originally placed beside one of God the Father in the clerestory as part of Christ's genealogy and dates from 1180. Unusually, Adam is depicted as a standing figure, in contrast to the traditional seated position. It was the consequence of Becket's murder that manifold gifts donated by the pilgrims to the shrine brought riches enough to sponsor the spate of stained glass that followed in their wake.

Beside the Genealogical Windows in the Nave and the Miracle Windows in the Trinity Chapel, there are the Bible Windows in the north Choir aisle; the Redemption Window in the Corona - with its Tree of Jesse Window; scenes from the lives of St Dunstan and St Alphege in the north Choir aisle clerestory, and the Rose Window in the north-east transept – among many others. Included in the Miracle Windows series is a portrait of Becket, said to have been done by someone who had known him: this might be interpreted as a living likeness of the saint.

In the Martyrdom the transept window survives the destruction by the iconoclasts. Known as the Royal Window, it figures Edward IV and his family at prayer: kneeling in file are the two young princes, Edward V and Duke of York - both fated to be murdered in the Tower. Of the five daughters, the eldest, Princess Elizabeth, stands out as being instrumental in bringing an end to the Wars of the Roses by marrying the first Tudor king, Henry VII.

Touching on the splendour of the cathedral, Erasmus, a visitor in Tudor times, commented on the wealth of items of gold, silver and precious stones on show, the surplus tucked away in cupboards. When invited to kiss the relics he declined, repulsed by the rotting parts of the anatomy proffered to his lips.

He was a great friend of the archbishop of the time, Wareham, who was the last in office before the Reformation. Twenty-six cartloads of valuables were carried away from the cathedral and purloined by Henry VIII for his coffers after the Dissolution.

Leaden Flask (Ampulla)

Source, the British Library

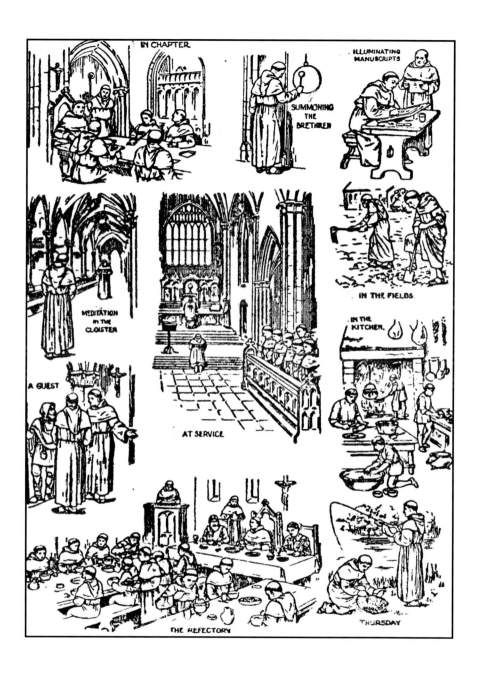

Monastic Life

Source, the British Library

Water from a Spring is Sprung

"Would you like to see the Water Tower?" I used to ask my groups, despite their courier's usual impatience to finish the tour (it was always obvious to me that the tour operators should have allotted more time to Canterbury in their itineraries). "Don't listen to her!" muttered some of her flock under their breath, eagerly following me as I led them out into the Great Cloister. "This way takes us to the exit – and the toilets," was always greeted with a sigh of relief.

On the way it gave me the opportunity to pop into the Chapter House to show them the magnificent ceiling of gilded and painted Irish bog oak. The interior was remodelled by Lote, Henry Yveley's pupil. The canopied stone seat at the eastern end was occupied by the prior. Stone benches for the monks flank the vast space, which is flooded with illumination from the large east window. (Its more recent stained glass show Henry VIII and Victoria, among other notable figures from history.) Here the monks conducted their daily business and listened to a rule of St. Benedict read out each morning.

Turning off the Great Cloister and through the Slype, site of the ancient library, with a brief stop to point out the stocky Norman pillars (their shafts decorated with variations of zig-zag and lozenge shapes) one comes upon the monks' Cloister: a greensward, formerly a herb garden that must have supplied the Infirmary ahead with potions and infusions, providing much needed medicines.

From the extent of the greensward a look back takes in the fine Water Tower, constructed by Wibert, prior from 1151 to 1167 (only the lower part remains of his work). He arranged for pipes to bring water from a spring near the city, which rose in the central column of the Water Tower to fill a large brass basin, enabling the monks to wash their face and hands on their way to nightly prayers. It is a water system that continues in modern form to the present day, benefitting the ladies responsible for flower arranging.

At the opposite end of the greensward rises the imposing vestige of the Necessarium, the lavatory that in its grandeur seated the whole monastic community. Underneath was a great ditch where excrement was sluiced away – urine being gathered for use in the Scriptorium for treating vellum.

Stained glass portrait of Becket, said to be by someone who remembered him.

Photo by Anne Jarvis, courtesy of the Dean and Chapter

Miscellany

There was never time to show my groups the roll of archbishops in office since Augustine that shines out on the west wall of the Nave. To pronounce the strange sounding names of the primates of the early Saxon years, such as Wulfred, Feologild, Ceolnoth, Plegmund, Wulfhelm – to name but a few – is somewhat of a challenge.

St Theodore of Tarsus stands out, not only as administrator, but also as a scholar, for, after his arrival from Greece in 668 A.D., he established a notable seat of learning. In fact, scholars from all over the world had been benefitting from the education to be had at Canterbury since 630 A.D.

Theodore can be said to have founded a school of such excellence that the reputation lives on in what later was to become King's (the monarch in question being Henry VIII who endowed it after the Dissolution of the Monasteries). The school is situated in the Precincts, some of whose schoolrooms are on the site of the monks' brewhouse and bakehouse, and reveal vestiges of the original structure inside the present buildings. From Archbishop Cranmer's creation for fifty scholars, a headmaster and an usher, it is today one of the most flourishing schools in the country.

Archbishop Theodore, with his friend, Abbot Hadrian, both fluent in languages, spread the scriptures and practiced logic. By his travels throughout the land, Theodore established the primacy's influence, and strengthened its supremacy.

The youthful Black Prince in the mid-1330's must have sat at the feet of his tutor, Prior Robert Hathbrand, imbibing happily the educative skills of the whole community. His lasting affection for Canterbury was such that he willed that the Cathedral of Christ Church be his eternal resting place.

Speaking of the Black Prince recalls a charming incident that happened to me in the cathedral:

Bee Boles in the old precinct wall by the site of the old medieval pond

Photo by Anne Jarvis, courtesy of the Dean and Chapter

A small boy approached, all bright-eyed and eager. His mother watched from a distance. She was obviously encouraging him to be self-reliant, yet at the same time keeping a protective eye on him. "Where is the Black Prince's tomb?" he asked. "Would you like me to show you?" "Yes, please!" When the recumbent figure came into view, "Oh, he's in bed!" the infant exclaimed, "He's at his prayers. He's saying: "Please God, don't kill me, don't kill me!" The quaintness of children can be as endearing as his was.

The cold winters in the monastery must have made life rather spartan for the boy prince – but he may have enjoyed the relative comfort of boarding in Meister Omers (a house in the Precincts for the entertainment of guests) or, perhaps, in the archbishop's palace. In contrast, the monks had to abide by the strict rules of St. Benedict, which eschewed comfort.

They were expected to leave the relative warmth of their beds during the night at one o'clock to process to the chapel in which the Night Offices of the Opus Dei were performed. For these nightly excursions they were issued with night shoes. Each pair was to last five years; of soft leather and fleecy lined, coming to above the knee – they were similar to the flying boots worn by airmen in World War II. They were highly prized, sometimes embroidered, and often being gifts from relatives, were a link with home.

Tenants on the cathedral estates sent in produce – and the prince's diet would have been enhanced by fish from the 12th century pond (the site of which was the area of the Precincts called The Oaks), and honey garnered from the "bee boles" – a row of niches in the wall by the pond to shelter straw bee-hives from the wind and rain, the honey being used in the making of mead. In the 1180's Archbishop Baldwin, a stern Cistercian, tried to reduce the monks' standard of living, rating it too high for a religious body.

The refectory and buttery were at the north end of the Cloister, whose ruins can be better guessed at from the Archdeacon's garden, with troughs for washing beforehand in the north Cloister aisle that still exist today. What remains of the kitchen is also evident in a corner of the Archdeacon's garden, which is entered from the Green Court - and the Cloister, when it is opened annually for a charitable cause.

In 1954 a new library was constructed on the site of the old that was bombed in World War II. The west wall of Lanfranc's dormitory remains part of it; this is the spot where Michael Stansfield, former Archivist, told me he had experienced a haunting. I had asked him if he had ever seen a ghost in the cathedral; he said that sometimes at the end of the day when all the staff had left and he was passing by the dormitory wall he would suddenly feel a presence.

Holst conducted his "Planets" in the Nave; the first performance of Eliot's drama "Murder in the Cathedral" took place in the Chapter House; and Masefield and Dorothy L. Sayers presented their plays in the cathedral during the early Canterbury Festivals.

Canterbury's Royal Castle in the early 12th century, a reconstruction.
It was never associated with warfare. In the late 11th century some
fractious monks in rebellion against Archbishop Lanfranc's appointment
of Wydo as Abbot of St Augustine's Abbey were inprisoned here; others
protested by sitting outside. Henry Yvele, the Royal Master Mason, did
repair work on the building in the 14th century.

Courtesy of the Canterbury Archaeological Trust

The mind boggles at the thought of all the eminent people who have trod the paving stones of Canterbury. During their stay the Emperor Charles V danced with Queen Catherine of Aragon, and Henry VIII with Charles's mother at the Archbishop's Palace. Henry V gave thanks for victory in Christ Church on his return from the battle of Agincourt; and the Black Prince led his captive, King John, here to celebrate mass. Countless others are mentioned in the course of this book.

It seems only yesterday that an advertisement caught my eye in St Stephen's Parish Magazine: the cathedral authority was prospecting for guides and assistants. Candidates were invited to enrol in a course about to start. As a successful applicant I was interviewed by Roy Ford, who was a retired headmaster, and for a few years Director of Visits in charge of the guides' office in Cathedral House. He was pleased that I spoke French and Italian. And so began many happy but intense years, first as assistant in a yellow sash, then as a guide with a yellow "palium" round the neck and coming to a V on the chest, with a badge. Assistants roam the cathedral attempting to be of help in enlightening visitors. Once an American – yes, it is usually an American who says the delightfully incongruous turn of phrase – accosted me with: "Say, are you ladies with sashes nuns?" As I always kept wallet and keys safely in a purse across my chest, it was quite usual to be asked: "Say, do you give change?" Assistants are always game for a chat among themselves, although knowing that even discreet huddles are frowned on – "Don't bunch!" could come a stern rebuke from a verger.

Being part of the cathedral community is thought of as quite an honour, which I was always aware of when being introduced to people by relatives, who would often add: "She guides at the cathedral". "Do you?" was the usual awed reply. The then Vicar of St Paul's, Cambridge, once breezily replied: "Oh, yes – G H Q" – which seems a good way of describing Mother Church.

The cosy routine of the early days of the Guides Office has given way to a very professional team busy at computers. No longer can Roy Ford burst into laughter at my first impressions, having long ago retired – impressions of a Barchester come to life. "When are you going to start guiding?" he often asked, needing another French and Italian speaking guide to draw on. But I hesitated, not feeling sufficiently genned up with facts.

Then one day I was pitched into it when one of the Italian speaking guides had to cancel her tour – would I step in? The group turned out to be a formidable bunch of Neapolitan teenagers – phew! But I did manage to get round. It was my baptism of fire!

First impressions are lasting: Barchester always comes to mind when I pass those Early Victorian french windows at the side of Cathedral House overlooking the Precincts. The Precincts is where I started my tour – thus I have come full circle; yet I cannot leave without pointing out other features in this section dubbed "Miscellany" (to include things I have inadvertently left out). Therefore let's explore the Precincts.

The exterior of the eastern half of the cathedral, built in Caen stone, is reminiscent of those in Normandy. Rounding the Corona (especially Norman in aspect) the fine Exchequer comes into view and the ruins of the Infirmary. It is not difficult to picture the scenario in pre-Reformation times – the aisles lined with beds where the sick monks were tended. Opposite, on the other side of the walk, is Choir House – and further on, the ruins of the Infirmary Chapel.

Visitors are possibly bemused by the mini buses parked in the Precincts near Choir House where the young choristers reside and which transport them daily to St Edmund's School for the continuation of their education.

On one occasion the guides enjoyed a conducted tour round Choir House to learn about the lives of these youngsters, who are looked after in a motherly and fatherly way by the housemaster and his wife, making it a home from home.

Top:
At the eastern end: the Trinity Chapel leading to the Corona; reminiscent of ecclesiastical buildings in Normandy. Note the fine Decorated window of St Anselm's Chapel; it was added in 1336 by Prior Oxenden

Bottom:
All that survives of the monks' exchequer built by Prior Eastry 1285-1331; part of the Corona is on the left. To the right looms Lanfranc's infirmary for sick monks cr. 1100, now in ruins.

Photos by Anne Jarvis, courtesy of the Dean and Chapter

There was a human touch – the beds in the dormitories strewn with teddy bears to cuddle. It was nice to see David Flood, the Organist, dealing out sweets at choir practice in reward for excellence. Each boy learns to play an instrument to which he applies himself after tea. We visitors were struck by the youthful aplomb shown us as the boys handed round refreshments and entertained us with their trip to the United States where they had performed and made recordings.

Christ Church Gate minus the present day sculpture of Christ.

Source the British Library

The south west entrance to Canterbury Cathedral with the Archbishop's Palace in the background.

Photo by Anne Jarvis, courtesy of the Dean and Chapter

The infallible aura of Canterbury Cathedral is felt by many a visitor on entering the Nave through the south-west door – and the Italians understand its religious spirituality to a degree. A detail which they find particularly simpatico concerns the Prayer Table, just into the north-east transept of the Western Crypt, alongside the Chapel of Our Lady Undercroft. It often prompted foreign visitors to add their prayers to others written and left ready for collection on the morrow, to be blessed at the altar during a service elsewhere in the cathedral. Visitors have come up to me from time to time and spoken of their feeling of a hallowed atmosphere in the place.

One of the loveliest features of the cathedral, where a particular peace is to be found is the Lady Chapel in the Martyrdom transept. Replacing the Norman apsidal Chapels of St Benedict and St Blaise, it was built with an early example of fan vaulting between 1448 and 1455.

"An evocative ancient door, north east ambulatory of the Choir.

Photo by courtesy of the Dean and Chapter

CHAUCER *(BUST IN THE GUILDHALL. LONDON.)*

THE CANTERBURY PILGRIMS

*Geoffrey Chaucer. c. 1340-1400. Through his **Canterbury Tales**, the first great literary work in English, Chaucer presents an invaluable picture of social life in the 14th century and symbolyzes the birth of the **Revival of Learning** which engendered a more enlightened civilization.*

Source the British Library

A dormitory at the Chequer of Hope Inn on the corner of High Street and Mercery Lane. In 1865 much of the building which housed galleries around the internal courtyard was destroyed by fire; its foundations now support the row of shops, including part of Debenham's department store on the left flank of Mercery Lane.

The Chequer of Hope, a vast courtyard inn, lodged pilgrims seeking miracles at Becket's shrine - until the demise of saintly relics at the Reformation left Canterbury empty of incomers, with the consequent loss of its erstwhile bustling humanity.

The hostelrie was one of a series that sprang up at the end of the 14th Century when veneration at the shrine was at its zenith. Under these rafters multitudes on pilgrimage huddled together in the sleep of the just.

Epilogue

After the nightly illumination is switched off – if we could roam the vast vaulted building that is Christ Church, our ears might just pick up echoes of the past. So intense was the drama in the history of this building that the aftermath of events has impregnated its very stones. The shades of medieval pilgrims pack the air – a scent of incense offsetting the heavy odour of unwashed bodies.

Hark to the tiny bells as the cover lifts off the shrine of Becket, their tinkling barely perceptible through the plainsong chant from the Choir.

The night shoes of the monks come shuffling through the gloom – giving way to Christmas 1170, when a tearful Becket, his congregation convulsed with sobs, reveals his grim premonition.

Then, as the knights' shouts rend the Martyrdom, the voice of Thomas comes echoing down the centuries: "I am no traitor, but a priest of God!"

Can you hear the sound of crashing glass beneath the blows of the iconoclasts, with cries of: "Off with his head!" as another saintly statue loses its crowning glory under the Reformation chop?

All played their part on the stage of history – as did those firewatchers on duty on the roof, who, when they flung back the incendiary bombs into the Precincts, became the saviours of the hour – tackling the Baedeker raids of the blitz with their bare hands.

In Canterbury's lifetime, many things by which English people had lived their lives have gone forever. Yet the Mother Church has survived traumatic changes, to stand proud and fair as a World Heritage Site, ever welcoming to present-day pilgrims.

Other books by the Author

A Jarvis Tapestry

The Early History of a Buckinghamshire Family from Tudor to Victorian Times.
Gloria Jarvis Smith tells the early history of her Buckinghamshire family through Tudor Yeoman Richard of Haddenham to Victorian Frederick William of Aylesbury, a founding father of Nelson Canada - not to mention yeoman Leonard of Gt. Hampden in his defiance of Charles I - and there's the hint of a distant knight, the sand of Normandy upon his feet. Interwoven with social history, it is mostly illustrated by the author, Gloria Jarvis Smith.

In hardback at £5.99 + £pp £2.00   ISBN 0-9543656-0-7

A Jarvis Tapestry Part II

The Story of an Edwardian Family of Aylesbury at Home and Beyond, Through the Twenties and Thirties to Modern Times
An Edwardian family of Aylesbury at home and beyond - through the Twenties, Thirties and Forties to modern times. In this sequel to Part I Gloria Jarvis Smith continues the story of her Buckinghamshire Jarvis kin - from beloved grandpa, Valentine Harry, to the present day. With illustrations by the author, Gloria Jarvis Smith, and Rupert Jarvis.

In hardback at £5.99 + £pp £2.00   ISBN 0-9543656-1-5

An Easel in the Family

"Fate, in taking me to Brussels, launched me into portraiture and the most prolific period of my creative work. One -woman exhibitions afforded me the happiest time of my life - certainly my painting life. In compiling this book I have been able to see much of my work coming together in one piece. It also forms a trilogy with the two histories of my family: A Jarvis Tapestry (parts 1 & 2)."

In hardback at £7.99 + £pp £2.00   ISBN 0-9543656-2-3

These books can be ordered by emailing:
sales@oysterpress.co.uk